CARING
for your new kitten

BY
DR. GORDON ROBERTS BVSC MRCVS

CHAPTER 1
introduction

What's the purpose of this book?

Are you about to get a little fuzzy friend? Or are they perhaps already with you? It's quite an interesting, exciting and daunting experience to add a brand new kitten to your home.. You can gain an insight into kitten behaviour by reading as much as you can about these interesting creatures. Gaining a better understanding of kittens is key to helping them get a fantastic start to life, be as healthy as possible and be happy as possible.

This book isn't about overloading your brain with complicated veterinary information. It's a simple, easy-to- read guide for new kitten owners. Hundreds of books could be written about kittens, but this one is all about going through the basic need-to-know details about caring for a new kitten. We'll start from the beginning, from choosing your feline friend, household precautions, tips on feeding and grooming, behavioural information, medical conditions, housetraining and much more.

The purpose of this information is to give a rough guide for any newbie kitten owner to understand the crucial steps to take to ensure their kitten is comfortable, happy and healthy. It also helps give you, as a pet owner, a greater awareness of the wellbeing of your kitten, how to care for them effectively and how to gain a greater knowledge of their behaviour. Kittens can't tell you exactly how content and well they feel, so it's vital to know as much as you can about them so you can recognise the signals. Many cat owners feel they have an improved and closer relationship with their cat once they learn more about taking care of them.

What do I need to be aware of before I start?

The first thing you need to know is that looking after a kitten is hard work – there's no point not being honest about that! Caring for any animal requires patience, understanding and a lot of love and your time. The second important thing is to remember these young kittens are by nature inquisitive and new to the world. They're not always going to do exactly what you want them to do! This is perfectly natural and you need to keep this in mind – punishment is by far the worst way to treat your kitten. They are beginners, much like you might be to having a kitten, and don't deserve nor benefit from being punished.

Though this book is a guide you must remember that every kitten is different, every home is different and every kitten owner is different. Though the guide gives you some valuable information and tips you have to remember that no book you ever read will be able to detail your exact circumstances and the exact character of your cat – those things are distinctive. That's why learning and enjoying your kitten's individual character is important so you can make the most out of this guide. As the saying goes , kittens are certainly not just for Christmas. Before you even take the first steps you have to think seriously about whether you have the time and the environment that's suitable for the needs of a cat. Kittens will need a little extra care and attention compared to the slightly more independent adult cat.

So, do you think you have what it takes? Do we have a caring, responsible cat lover reading this ready to get the ball rolling? If so, congratulations! You won't regret it. Having a kitten isn't easy, but it's a deeply rewarding experience – let's get started!

CHAPTER 2
choosing your kitten

Before you start looking at where to find your ideal kitten, you need to figure out which kind of kitten you want. Do you want a female or a male? Which breed do you want? Do you want a pedigree or not? We can't answer these questions for you because it's entirely up to you. If you don't mind, then problem solved! If you do, then here's a little information on gender, neutering, pedigrees and breeds you might find useful…

A female kitten just as a pet: Show signs of maturing at approximately six months old. From around this age she will start a kind of cat puberty and will begin to go into season on and off for around eight months of each year. The chances of pregnancy can be quite high, particularly if she is allowed outdoors. Neutering is strongly recommended because of this and for other health reasons and particularly if you just want her as a pet and not for breeding purposes. Speak to your vet about neutering and when could be the right time to do it.

A male kitten just as a pet: Again, males show maturity signs around six months of age. From this age they may show signs of spraying, fighting and wandering. If you have him just for the purpose of a pet then it's strongly advised to get him neutered and these behaviours are likely to ease. Speak to your vet about neutering and when could be the right time to do it.
A note on neutering: Don't be concerned about neutering. It sounds cruel, but it's not at all. It's safe and doesn't affect your cat's quality of life but can improve their health.   It willprevent numerous unplanned litters, prevent aggressive behaviour and generally help your cat's wellbeing. It's strongly advised by vets and you're vet will welcome the opportunity to discuss this with you.

Kittens and pedigree kittens for breeding: If you pick a male or female kitten for future breeding then you must be aware of the differences in behaviour an unneutered cat will have compared to a neutered one. Females for breeding, otherwise known as queens, will be on heat occasionally and will become very needy and vocal.

If you're keeping her for breeding, especially if she's a pedigree, you should keep her indoors to prevent unwanted pregnancy. Males for breeding, otherwise known as studs, will be more likely to spray around the house, go off to explore and get into fights.

Breeds

The breed of a kitten depends on whether you want a pedigree or not. Moggies are cheaper to buy, but still cost the same as pedigrees when it comes to food, vet expensesetc. Pedigrees are more costly to purchase and sometimes can cost a little more in pet insurance. Some people want moggies, some want pedigrees. When it comes to choosing a breed of kitten, nobody can tell you which one to go for – it's your choice! Some breeds have characteristics assigned to them, but the best thing about cats is each one has their own individual character to enjoy and we simply cannot predict how they will be, particularly when they grow up into adult cats.

We can't list every single breed, so here are just a few examples of traits and breeds to give you an idea. Moggies and random-bred cats are harder to describe as they come from such a mix. It's unlikely you'll be disappointed with whatever you choose. Cats are charismatic regardless!

Short and medium haired: American Shorthair, Siamese, Tonkinese, British Shorthair, Abyssinian, Russian Blue, Scottish Fold, Manx, Exotic Shorthair, Burmese, etc.

Long haired: Birman, Norwegian Forest Cat, Turkish Angora, Turkish Van, Persian, Ragdoll, Maine Coon, Himalayan, Siberian, etc.

Sociable: Bengal, Siamese, Abyssinian, Maine Coon, Scottish Fold, Siberian, Persian, Ragdoll, Sphynx, Manx, Tonkinese, Oriental, Exotic Shorthair, Russian Blue, Burmese, etc.

Active: Ocicat, Birman, Abyssinian, Siberian, Tonkinese, Sphynx, Bengal, Turkish Van, Manx, Egyptian Mau, Cornish & Devon Rex, Siamese, Oriental, Scottish Fold, Russian Blue, etc.

Affectionate: Siamese, Persian, Norwegian Forest Cat, Ragdoll, Scottish Fold, American Shorthair, Birman, Bengal, Tonkinese, Devon & Cornish Rex, Burmese, Turkish Van, Egyptian Mau, Maine Coon, Sphynx, Exotic Shorthair, etc.

Lap lovers: Ragdoll, Tonkinese, Egyptian Mau, Devon Rex, Ocicat, Sphynx, Siberian, Cornish Rex, Burmese, Siamese, British Shorthair, American Shorthair, Maine Coon, etc.

What things should I look out for when choosing a kitten?

Some things you need to be aware of about the kitten choosing process is how to check the gender of a kitten and how to notice when a kitten is healthy.

Checking gender: Gently lift the tail. At the top you'll find the anus and just a little below you'll see the genitalia is a vertical slit for a female. For a male it will be further down and the opening is more circular. After about six weeks a male kitten will be easier to notice because the testicles will begin to show.

Signs of a healthy kitten:

- They are at least eight weeks old when you home them – they must not leave their mother before this time from a development point of view
- They feel and look a reasonable weight
- Clear eyes with no discharge or abnormal appearance
- A healthy, good condition coat with no sign of fleas or bald patches
- A healthy, dry tail and a clean and normal looking rear area
- Clean ears with no signs of mites
- Energetic and normal behaviour

Any signs of poor health, lethargy, sores, poor mobility, discharges, signs of mites, parasites or fleas, vomiting, diarrhoea or other abnormal issues should be avoided. If you are concerned about a kitten or litter of kitten's welfare from the way they are treated, their living conditions or their health then please contact specialist animal welfare organisations such as the RSPCA. Our next chapter will discuss how to find a reputable breeder and what to do next. Here you may find the answers to further questions about choosing a kitten, kitten health, rescue kittens, precautions, rules to adhere to, etc.

CHAPTER 3
how to find a reputable breeder

You need to work out where to get your kitten from. This often leaves a lot of people scratching their heads in confusion as it's a process where you need to find out lots of factors. You just need to be wary of people and places that don't play by the rules and you must try to do enough research into safe sources.

Firstly, you need to have made a decision about which breed of cat you want and ensure you have the right supplies for them when they get home. You also need to ensure you find out enough about the people or place you adopt your kitten from and the kitten itself. The advice on signs of a healthy kitten in the previous chapter is helpful when choosing and collecting the kitten.

Things to find out before adopting your kitten:

- How old are they?
- Can I see the mother?
- Are they micro chipped?
- Are they neutered?
- Do they have a medical condition?
- Are they healthy, been checked recently by a vet and have their own health report?
- Have they been vaccinated? When are they due to be?
- If there is a cost, how much is it?
- What kind of character does the kitten have?
- Are they a registered breeder and can they prove it?
- Does the pedigree come with official documentation?
- Do the breeders have any referrals/recommendations?
- Are there any hereditary health problems this breed is susceptible to?
- Are their living conditions clean and spacious with signs of being well cared for?
- Are their parents healthy? Is there any proof such as an annual vet check-up report?

Rescue/cat home kittens: Lots of people like adopting a kitten from a cat home – random bred and purebred. Here you might find orphaned, abandoned or disabled kittens as well as kittens who have been treated poorly and have been moved on to a safer environment. These little critters all need rehoming and it can be a really beautiful experience bringing love, care and attention into their lives again. If you plump for this option you can find the official websites of a reputable organisation or shelter and check for any local branches. You need to be aware of how the kitten lived before it was rescued as this may be a reason behind any health or behavioural problems. Get them checked by a vet as soon as you adopt them.

Rehoming advertisements: Newspapers and websites often have ads from kitten owners who need to rehome their pet for whatever reason. Lots of animal organisations have adoption sections where people are free to place their own ad to find a home for their kitten. Always speak to the owners directly and remember to check the kitten's health when you see them. Seeing them with their mother is also a good indication of their wellbeing. Again, we recommend getting them checked by a vet once you adopt them.

Breeders: A safer and more trustworthy breeder should be registered. Checking to see if they have any decent referrals is also helpful. Going to a registered and experienced breeder is the best way to obtain a pedigree. Your pedigree kitten should come with registered pedigree documentation. Various websites list good cat breeders as well as magazines. Visiting cat-related events such as cat shows can also link you to recommended breeders, breeder clubs and similar feline themed organisations or associations who may have information. Going through a friend is also a more trusted route to take.

Disabled kittens: Another rewarding option is adopting a disabled kitten. Many can be found at cat shelters and need a safe and understanding home. You just need to be aware about their medical condition and implications of this, whether it's making adjustments around the home, knowing how to administer medications or having the budget to cover the veterinary bills and/or insurance. A visit to the vet is strongly recommended soon after you adopt them.

Pet stores: The conditions in pet stores are not always satisfactory and it is generally said these are not the best places to find a healthy kitten. The spaces they are kept in are often too small and many kittens come from unknown mothers and unhealthy environments where risk of being unvaccinated or having diseases is higher – you have no idea where the kittens come from and how they were treated.

Catteries/kitten mills: Again avoid these. Conditions are often poor and overcrowded, kittens are often sold far too young when they need to be with their mother, and mothers are often expected to have litter after litter. Poorer health, mites and fleas are more likely and kittens are more likely also to have had less human interaction.

Important precautions:

- Allow time to interact with the litter of kittens
- Check the chosen kitten's eyes, mouth, ears, tail, fur, weight and behaviour
- Also check the conditions the kitten has been living in
- Poor health, poor treatment and poor conditions should be reported to places such as the local council or the RSPCA

- Watch out for 'backyard breeders' – they are normally unregistered, sell kittens too young, leave the kitten with a poor sense of human interaction and don't take into consideration genetic pitfalls such as inherited behavioural or medical conditions
- Ensure you get all necessary documentation (pedigree certificates, health records, micro chipping documents, etc.)
- Ensure the mother is in good health
- Depending on the kitten's age, be aware of if they have been vaccinated
- Refer to the 'Signs of a healthy kitten' and 'Things to find out before adopting your kitten' during your time visiting your potential kitten

CHAPTER 4
introducing your kitten to a safe and suitable home

The kitten is finally chosen and about to arrive in their brand new home. There are a number of things you can do to make this process as comfortable as possible. Kittens coming to a completely new environment may be a little stressed or anxious at first, especially if they have come straight from their mother and brothers and sisters. So, taking a few of the following steps can make a big difference to what your kitten will consider a sudden, daunting experience.

The essentials must be ready: Obviously you need a decent kitten litter tray, a good stock of litter, some kitten food, food and water bowls, a warm and comfortable bed, plenty of stimulating toys and a travel container for when your kitten needs to be taken to the vet.

Special adjustments for disabled kittens: If you're bringing home a kitten with a disability or pre-existing condition you need to be aware of what adjustments to make around the house – e.g. if the kitten has problems with mobility you can purchase specialist litter trays and ramps to help them access everything they need to. Special toys can be bought according to the disability and extra precautions need to be made around the home so accidents can't happen.

Take them to the vet: Register them with the nearest vet and get them an appointment for a health check-up to ensure they are doing well. Your vet can give you valuable advice and undertake the necessary checks and vaccinations your kitten will need over the months.

Smaller spaces to begin with: Letting your kitten out of its travel box into a massive unknown house can be too much. Keeping your beloved kitten in one room to begin with will ease this problem. Keep them there for a couple of days and see how they cope in larger rooms or sections of the house. Gradual steps are better than drastic ones. Keep their essentials in this room (litter tray, food, water, bed, toys, etc.) Remember to keep the litter tray in the same place so they don't get confused as to where they should go to the toilet.

Cautious with other pets: Your kitten isn't going to want, for example, a big dog invading their space to begin with. Particularly if they've never met one before! After a few days of being kept separate you should introduce them in short intervals and always be around to supervise If needed you can keep them apart for a short period.

Handle with care: Be gentle and teach any younger people in the household to handle your kitten gently too – they also need to be aware of over-handling. Kittens are adorable, so it's easy for children to want to cuddle and hold them all the time, but over-handling isn't comfortable and kittens need lots of sleep and rest without the constant hassle. Handle in moderation.

Give them time to explore: Your kitten is trying to discover their new surroundings. This could make them anxious or shy and they may hide away. Let them explore and don't be too harsh on them or they may become even more scared than they already are. Keep an eye on them to begin with just in case they crawl into your dishwasher or somewhere equally as dangerous! Move them away from unwanted areas and take them to comfortable, safe places.

Don't buy just any cat toy: Buy ones that are especially designed for kittens. Some cat toys could have small parts posing a choking risk as well as toys with sharp edges that could cause a serious injury. You probably have noticed by now that precautions for kittens are much like they are with small children – avoid toys that are choking hazards. Larger, softer toys are preferable but not the ones with long fibres as these could come off and your kitten will more than likely swallow them.Remember Kittens, as with all young sters, need lots of stimulation.

Don't socially isolate your kitten: A curious and somewhat scared kitten stepping foot in a new home will need reassurance and lots of social attention to make them feel more comfortable and safe. Also think about what it will be like for them when the house is empty. Will they have enough toys to play with? Enough places to feel safe and secure, so they can relax and observe? Are they quite clingy and have a risk of being lonely? A kitten with separation anxiety isn't a happy one. You may even want to get more than one kitten so they have each other for company!

One extremely important preparation for a new kitten is 'kitten proofing' your home. This isn't just for their arrival, but ensures their safety throughout their lives, so it's very important to read the following advice and bear it in mind…

Household hazards: Your home needs to be as safe as possible for such a vulnerable, little creature. Kittens love to explore and go all over the place, so pay some attention to the potential hazards you could have around the home. Examples include keeping chemicals in high cupboards, removing small objects from a kitten's reach, covering cables a kitten could chew, keep medications away in high cupboards, keep potentially toxic foods stored away, remove any poisonous plants, etc. Anything a kitten can choke on, drink or eat out of curiosity, chew or play with and so on, that is not safe needs to be stored in unreachable places. Remember very simple household objects such as plants or human foods can be seriously poisonous. Even if you left your kitten with a piece of string it would be risky, they could swallow it, or get twisted up as they roll and play and could suffocate themselves with it. When it comes to hazards treat your kitten as if it were a human baby.

Hopefully, you'll be a caring owner and over time will learn about your kitten's needs. As long as you remember to be safe and be vigilant over your kitten's wellbeing everything should be fine. Your vet is always available to discuss any concerns or queries you have.

CHAPTER 5
essential everyday care for new kittens

Your kitten is starting to get used to their new home, but are you getting used to being a great kitten owner? Simple steps from feeding to grooming are essential to get right. In this chapter, we'll take a look at how to adopt a good feeding routine and effective grooming techniques to ensure your kitten's day-to-day needs are catered for well.

Feeding – A kitten's favourite activity

Cats adore meal times. Kittens are forever growing and developing and need lots of food – they are simply mad about it! So, it's important to get it done the right way. Too many people overfeed or underfeed their cats. Some people even feed their kitten the wrong foods. Problems that start from such a young age have an impact on a kitten's development. They need a healthy, balanced and suitable diet or their wellbeing can suffer.

Firstly, you need to find a reputable pet food brand that has foods targeted for kittens. Giving your kitten adult cat food may cause upset. Kitten food will be easier to digest and contain the essential ingredients to aid growth. You can choose from either tinned or dried, though a combination of both is better.

Secondly, your kitten will need to be fed a little more often than an adult cat. An adult cat ideally has two meals a day, but a growing kitten will need around four or five small meals a day. Some cat food brands will instruct you on the packaging, so read these as they can vary from one brand to another. Always give your kitten access to the food bowl and the water bowl. It's essential your kitten is well hydrated, especially if your kitten is eating dried food..

When your kitten has reached the starting signs of maturity at around six months old you can start thinking about adapting the feeding routine to an adult one – two larger meals a day. Some kittens may wish to continue having multiple small meal times a day and this is fine to continue for a short while. As cats naturally like to engage in pick-me-up snacking you should leave a bowl of kitten biscuits out they can eat from at their leisure. Just be careful not to feed or top-up food too much.

Each individual kitten will have their own appetite – you might have one who isn't bothered or you might have one who is greedy! You need to learn how your kitten takes their food and feed them accordingly. Obviously, don't go overboard or give too little. Some kittens may reject their meals and be fussy. If so, wait a while and you may find when they're hungry they'll eat it! If it persists then try another brand of kitten food and always keep a bowl of kitten biscuits out as a reserve. Kittens that always leave behind a portion of food are probably being given too much. Your vet can advise on diet and will need to check your kitten's weight on occasion.

Things to avoid:

- Avoid feeding foods that contain skin or bones
- Avoid giving your kitten extra portions when it is not needed
- Avoid not paying enough attention to your kitten's appetite
- Avoid leaving meat out all day –biscuits are fine
- Avoid chilled foods – room temperature foods are best
- Avoid serving their food in bowls that haven't be thoroughly washed beforehand
- Avoid giving your kitten a non-meat diet – meat is a vital element
- Avoid giving your kitten human foods as some can be toxic and/or cause sickness

Advice on weaning: Normally, if you get a kitten from a reputable source weaning won't be necessary – weaning is normally done around four to six weeks of age and kittens should only be rehomed from eight weeks onwards. Kittens bought from a pet shop may require weaning as they are more likely to be used to their mother's milk instead solid kitten foods. You should therefore avoid getting a kitten that hasn't been 100% weaned off milk as a sudden change to diet can cause upset. Another reason your kitten needs weaning is because it has been separated from its mother too early. Weaning onto solid food should be done on a small and gradual basis with foods mushed down for easier digestion. Any concerns, problems or queries are best dealt with by your vet.

A well groomed kitten

A feline with a shiny, healthy coat is in good condition because they have an owner who gives them a good diet and grooms them well. Some kittens come from breeds with notoriously long fur and others from short fur. Regardless of length your kitten will benefit hugely from being regularly groomed. Longhaired kittens will need grooming more than shorthairs – some may even require grooming on a daily basis.

The benefits of grooming:

Healthier coat: Your kitten's coat will be softer, shinier and generally in better condition.

No clumps: It reduces the chances of knotted or clumped fur leaving the fur smooth and untangled.

More grooming, less moulting: Kittens will moult according to the seasons and this can get just about everywhere – especially on clothing. Grooming them will help shed coats and brush away loose fur so it doesn't end up on your favourite attire!

Avoiding hairballs: When your kitten grooms themselves looser fur can often be ingested causing hairballs in the stomach. Your cat can cough these up or even become ill from the build-up of fur in their stomach, so grooming looser fur away can reduce this from happening.

Could help allergies: Someone in your household who is allergic to cats may find that when you groom the kitten and get rid of looser fur less of it they get less irritation.

Lessens dandruff: Yes, kittens can get dandruff too! A regular grooming routine will help reduce levels of dandruff.

Good for checking skin: Brushing your kitten will give you the opportunity to check their fur and their skin for any abnormalities such as lumps, sores, fleas and so on.

Bonding with you – grooming will help your kitten bond with you and will become quality down time for the two of you. Very relaxing for you both and has health benefits too.

Various pet shops have a variety of grooming equipment to choose from. Start off by getting a couple of different combs, particularly a flea comb, and a softer brush. Grooming needs for kittens will vary and depend on the breed and length of hair.

Shorthaired kittens – Don't need as much grooming as longer haired kittens and often perform the majority of their grooming requirements themselves. It's still advised to regularly and gently brush them to smoothened out the coat and get rid of loose furs. You can groom down the length of the body, but avoid the face and around the eyes and other similarly delicate areas. Cotton wool buds are effective in the gentle cleaning of any mucus on the face.

Longhaired kittens – To avoid matting you should groom longhaired kittens on a daily basis. Not grooming regularly leaves matted fur that can be uncomfortable and unhealthy for your kitten. Brush every day gently getting to the whole length of the body. Time spent on brushing should be longer than that taken grooming a shorthaired kitten. Combing longer fur is also recommended to avoid tangling. If your kitten's fur tangles anywhere then you will know you aren't grooming thoroughly enough and in all the necessary areas. Avoid delicate areas such as the face and eyes. Mucus accumulating on the face can be gently cleaned away with cotton wool buds.

What if my kitten's coat moults excessively?

If you notice your kitten's fur moults far too much then this could be a sign of poor health. Excessive moulting, duller coats or any other abnormal problems from the fur such as patches of baldness should be investigated by your vet. A coat in poor condition can be improved drastically with a healthier diet and regular, gentle grooming routines.

Do I need to clip my kitten's claws?

Adult indoor cats are probably the most likely candidates for occasional claw clipping. Kittens, however, don't always need their claws clipped because their level of activity every day should be enough to keep them at a desirable length. If, however, they are starting to damage furniture or cause you and others harm you should consider some housetraining. You can also provide lots of toys and scratching posts as a means to wear down sharp and long claws. If you really feel the need to give them a clip you should ask your vet for advice and they can show you how to clip claws properly without causing your kitten any harm.

CHAPTER 6
kitten development – step by step

Observing your kitten's development week by week is a good way of understanding their biology, their needs, their character and what to expect from them. This chapter is an approximate and simple guide explaining what could be happening as your kitten grows and when they are ready for certain things.

If your cat has had a litter of kittens then it's best to start from week 1 because you will witness the very first stages of a kitten's life. If you have rehomed a kitten you should start from week 8 as this is the minimum age a kitten can safely be separated from its mother and be rehomed.

Week 1:
At the end of the first week you'll notice the kitten's weight will increase to approximately two times that of its birth weight. They will suckle from their mother for long periods of time, up to four hours a day. Mobility is limited, and their eyes are closed, but kittens may still show signs of movement such as pulling themselves across the floor. Their prime activity is sleep, which they do for around 16 hours of the day. By the week's end they are more capable of keeping warm, but try to keep them comfortable with plenty of towels or blankets in a large bed or cardboard box.

Week 2:
Suckling reduces to around three hours a day. Mobility increases. At some point you should expect to see their eyes and ears beginning to open and the first teeth start to come through. The eyes start off blue in colour and months later the actual eye colour will develop.

Week 3:
Suckling reduces to around two hours a day. You'll notice the kittens starting to use their limbs more effectively by walking - they will be a little unsteady doing so at this stage. Better mobility means they will start to play with each other and shadow their mother's actions. They'll also start to progress a sense of smell. At this point they will need some human interaction briefly every day which will help to get them used to being handled.

Week 4:
By this stage the weight has increased twice as much and the kittens have full hearing capabilities. Kittens may start to become hungrier due to the mother making less milk and this could lead to them sampling solid cat food. Though soiling accidents will still occur, the kittens by now will have shadowed their mother's behaviour with the litter box and will be mastering how to use it themselves. Be sure to have several litter boxes around the home so your kittens aren't "caught short"! More teeth will begin to come through and interaction and playtime between the kittens and their mother will increase. At this point you can also gently supervise and teach the kittens about how to behave well – a chapter later in this book will go into detail on how to do this.

Week 5 to 7:
More weight will be gained and will gradually continue to gain until around six months of age. Kittens continue to successfully copy their mother, with the last remaining teeth coming through and an increased interest in eating solid foods. They may still wish to suckle from their mother for a short while. Each individual kitten is now capable of keeping warm by themselves. Kittens should be learning about how to handle certain situations and enough human interaction and interaction with other cats and animals is helpful in order for your kitten to learn to adjust.

Week 8 to 9:
Normally this is the minimum expected age you can adopt or rehome a kitten. This is because by now the kitten should be fine with doing things away from its mother and they won't need their mother's milk – they should be completely weaned on to solid kitten food. They need plenty of toys and interaction with you as the desire to exercise their muscles and be active is increased.

Between month 3 to 6:
After week nine onwards your kitten's social and play abilities will be at their best. Teeth will fall out and be replaced by adult ones. Though signs of maturity show at six months, some females will go into season for the first time a little earlier and can even become pregnant, so be careful and speak to your vet about when the suitable time will be for neutering.

From month 6 up until 12:
Maturity begins at around six months or later.
Males at this point can then show signs of fighting and spraying. Weight and coats will grow a little more over this time. Again, speak to your vet about the possibility of neutering and when.

If any problems arise during this exciting developmental process you should speak to your vet. Some problems and medical issues will be addressed in a later chapter for your reference, but any suspicion of difficulties or poor health needs to be addressed by your vet first hand.

CHAPTER 7
socialisation

Cats and kittens are social creatures and require interaction just like a dog would. In fact, socialisation right from the word go is vital for kitten development and learning. Socialisation isn't just about being social, but about getting used to surroundings and situations and learning how to react and behave.

When will my kitten start socialising?

Kittens show signs of socialisation from only a few weeks old and this socialisation learning period can go on for around three months. From three weeks of age they will start to move, their ears and eyes will have opened and they will have the chance to notice their mother's behaviour. From then on the kitten will start being playful with their litter siblings and will also require human interaction so they can learn early on how to get used to humans.

What kind of things is my kitten learning about during this time?

Through the learning process your kitten will be exposed to things that could potentially be scary to them - objects around the house, other animals, people or house visitors, noises and so on. They will need to be introduced gradually so they can familiarise themselves with things at their own pace, but retreat to a calmer environment if it gets too much. Once they learn how to cope fully the objects, people or animals will be considered normal to the kitten.

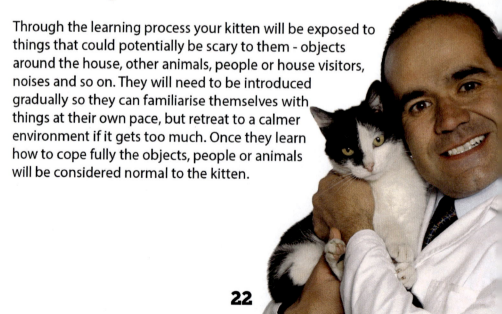

How can I help train my kitten with this?

After reading this chapter a chapter on housetraining will follow with more detailed steps on how to help your kitten and to regulate their behaviour. Read through it and try it out.

What is the best way to socialise with kittens?

A kitten will learn to familiarise with humans and interact with humans if they've been handled from a young age. After about three weeks you can gradually start to interact with the kitten. Start with a daily pick up for a few minutes each time and then increase the amount and time over the next few days. Just be careful not to overtire them. Gently picking them up for a brief moment is best to begin with and do this by gently holding under the body with one hand and holding the hind legs with the other. Once you know the kitten is comfortable you can continue, you must support their hind quarters. Don't pick them up by the scruff as this can be harmful. It's a good idea to teach children to handle kittens correctly, too. Think of it as a learning process for all of you, including your kitten. After a time when you notice your kitten is more relaxed with handling, you can introduce gentle stroking and then light and gentle play with safe toys. Avoid toys with small parts or string as they are a choking risk.

How do kittens socialise?

Remember the kitten is learning, so they're a beginner and are trying to take in the world around them with lots of distractions. Because of this they might not know how to socialise straight away and will normally try and imitate their mother. Socialisation would probably start out between the kitten and its siblings and mother. This is why kittens should never be separated from their mother and litter too early. They need to adapt and learn how to interact with other cats. It won't be long before the kitten will play and wrestle with their mother and siblings which they should be allowed to do. A mother can actually be a good teacher, particularly when your kitten does something naughty and the mother is there to tell them off.

When it comes to other animals you should never assume your kitten will act badly. Introduce them slowly in a calm atmosphere – it's important you are calm too. Introduce in little chunks and also supervise them during this time so you can reassure your pets and tell them if they misbehave towards each other. Calm and gentle introductions will help your kitten get used to other pets. The next few chapters on housetraining and understanding kitten behaviour will help you notice how and why your kitten behaves and reacts in certain ways and how you can regulate it.

How do I know if there is a problem with my kitten's socialisation?

If they are only a few weeks old then be patient. They are still learning and could probably do with a bit more interaction from you, their mother and litter. If, however, you have an older kitten who shows signs of poor social skills, ie they are timid and shy away, or are overly agressive, poor awareness or poor behaviour you should think about what could be the problem. Is your kitten anxious or scared? Do they hide when the dog runs in? Was the kitten taken away from its mother too soon? Try and make their environment calmer, quieter and easier to be in. Allow other pets to interact with the kitten in a calm and controlled manner. Comfort your kitten and spend time socialising with them with handling, affection and play time. Details on behavioural and medical problems are detailed in a later chapter along with housetraining tips including de-sensitisation and counterconditioning – in fact, these two factors could be a great help in easing your kitten into a more comfortable and sociable frame of mind. If you're really concerned you can always speak to your vet.

CHAPTER 8
housetraining your kitten

Gently training your kitten is a good way for them to learn how to behave around the house, with other animals and with humans. Here a few of the most common problems are listed and how each one can be improved with basic housetraining methods. Don't feel too daunted by the word 'training'. It sounds like a long rigmarole, but it can be quite simple and effective, so it's worth investing some time and patience .

Before you start – Training is all about patience, understanding, being gentle, being fair and realising your kitten is a beginner. You should never punish your kitten when they do something you think is wrong.

Punishment actually has the exact opposite effect. Shouting, neglect or physical punishment is cruel and will only cause your kitten to be very scared of you, hide away, be stressed or anxious and in some cases even cause them considerable harm.

Litter box training

Naturally kittens will eliminate around the house. After a few weeks they will start to follow their mother around and notice what she does, including going to the litter tray. Kittens will imitate their mother, but it could take some time for them to fully use the litter tray every time, and get used to realising that even though their paws are in the tray their rear end may not be!

Remember kittens will not have as much control over their bowel and bladder as older cats, so if don't have easy nearby access to the litter tray, you could be asking for trouble. If you've adopted a kitten the chances are they are already at an age where they know how to use the litter tray.

Here are some tips for effective litter box training:

- Have a few litter boxes around the house instead of one, but keep in the same place
- By now you should be recognising the signs when your kitten needs to use the litter tray
- Make sure the litter boxes are small ones designed for kittens for ease of access
- Keep the litter trays away from their eating and sleeping areas and away from distractions
- Take your kitten to the tray soon after they eat a meal
- Gently drag their paw through the litter to encourage the digging motion
- Don't change the litter every time after each elimination as the scent is a good way to signal the kitten to eliminate there
- Praise and reward a kitten you see using the tray with a treat
- Allow the kitten to make their own way out so they learn how to get in and out themselves
- By now you should be recognising the signs when your kitten needs to use the litter tray
- If you see your kitten eliminating out of the box take them to the tray immediately so they associate the two together
- Don't give up – it may take a while, but it's worth it!

A kitten? Taking commands? As if!

Training a kitten to respond to commands isn't that unusual. It's a common misconception that teaching commands is something you just do with dogs. Kittens can respond well by familiarising themselves with their name, your tone of voice and particular words assigned to an action. It's great for when you want them to stop doing something naughty, leave or enter a room, get down from restricted surfaces and so on.

Here are some tips on how to train your kitten to react to commands the right way:

- Call their name in a high pitch tone so their ears will prick up and you have their attention
- Don't use their name out of anger as this will stop them from wanting to go near you when you call their name in future
- Say their name and a command such as "come here" while crouching down holding a treat – repeat this often until they get used to it
- Allow the kitten to come over and give them the treat
- When they do so use words of encouragement and praise – maybe stroke them too
- After a short while you can try using the same name, "come here" command and same actions without using a treat – this may take some time to achieve!
- For kittens jumping up onto prohibited surfaces you could invest in a 'cat tree' as an alternative way your cat can climb and view the room from above
- Use an assertive, but not aggressive tone of voice when you see your kitten on prohibited surfaces or areas/rooms
- Use a command word such as "down" or "out" and use neutral body language to help them understand what you are saying – point to the floor, clap your hands or wag your finger
- Use treats to entice your kitten away from the surfaces or areas and on to/into the areas they can be in or climb on (e.g. the cat tree)
- Be careful using treats too often as your kitten may learn that they get a treat by jumping onto surfaces and the unwanted behaviour will get worse
- Using something to squirt water at your kitten to get them down is a popular option for many, but you might be risking startling and scaring them which isn't helpful for their wellbeing or development, especially during the socialisation period
- Assign certain tones, words and body language for when they do wrong and when they do right and use them often so they can distinguish from the two, e.g. saying "no" in a deeper and drawn out tone a few times over while wagging your finger at their nose or clapping when your kitten is naughty or "good boy/girl" in a higher, cheery tone a few times over while stroking your kitten when they're good

Scratching or biting – ouch!

It's not enjoyable when you're playing or handling your kitten and they bite or scratch at you. It makes you think they could attack at any moment. There are ways you can try and ease this aggression in your kitten and show them responding in this way is wrong. Many kittens can become aware of when they dig their claws in or sink their teeth in too much from play fighting with their siblings or mother. The attacked cat will yelp and their reaction will show the attacker they went too far. Some kittens are more prone to fighting and being aggressive, such as unneutered males.

Here are some tips on how to ease aggressive behaviour:

- If it's a male and they are old enough consider getting him neutered as this can help
- If your kitten bites or claws during play immediately stop playing with them, point at their nose and say in a deep and assertive voice "no" a few times
- Put a halt to play time if your kitten gets aggressive and go away and ignore your kitten for a short period – the sudden lack of attention will help them associate clawing and biting with play time being over
- Avoid dangling your feet, hands or fingers in your kitten's face as this will encourage them to want to play with them
- Take extra care when children play with the kitten and teach the children not to aggravate or entice the kitten to bite their fingers
- Use safe toys during play so kittens learn to play fight them instead of your hands or feet
- A crafty and sudden nip or scratch from your kitten should prompt you to remove your hands away from the kitten quickly and avoid contact – also give a "no" command
- Avoid any rewarding behaviour towards your kitten if they are biting or scratching – giving them a toy when they attack you may seem like a good idea, but your kitten might assume you are rewarding their aggression
- A kitten scratching or gnawing at furniture should be given a firm and repeated "no" accompanied by a hand clap or finger wag
- Give your kitten a scratching post as an alternative to scratching and gnawing furniture
- Put treats and alluring scents on the places your kitten is allowed to scratch

Meeting and behaving nicely with other animals

This is important if you have other pets in your household. You want your kitten to get on well with the other pets and for every animal to be happy. Many kittens will take to other animals or other cats well, but sometimes you might need to take some steps to ensure everybody is behaving nicely towards each other or your house will become an uncomfortable place for your pets.

Here are a few tips on teaching your kitten and other pets to behave with one another:

- Considering neutering, if you put two or more kittens together as they reach maturity male kittens in particular will fight each other,
- Naturally, putting a male and female kitten together, even if brother and sister, could produce an early litter
- Before introducing your kitten to other pets you should set aside a few days where they can be kept in a calm room in the house and adapt to their new environment without fear
- Also allow your kitten to become familiarised with you first, they will be more confident if you are there
- Allow the kitten time to be introduced casually to the other pet
- Supervise the introduction and try to be calm and avoid alarming the animals
- Allow each animal to sniff and investigate each other as long as there is no fighting or aggression
- Ensure the new kitten has somewhere they can retreat to if it all gets too much
- Show all your pets equal attention and affection
- Encourage, reward and praise both parties when they behave well with each other
- Use assertive telling off words if one of them gets naughty
- If you're introducing your kitten to an older dog perhaps try keeping them on a leash for the first few meetings
- Don't leave the two parties alone together at the beginning
- If they show no signs of adjusting to each other's company over the space of a few months you may need to speak to a behaviourist or consider the possibility they may be incompatible and must be separated permanently

Socialisation training

Your kitten may benefit from a bit of light training during the socialisation period where your kitten learns to adapt to social situations and environments. Lots of the adapting will be down to your kitten to achieve over time, but you can always take steps to help them along the way.

Some of these include:

- Teach your kitten how to get used to being handled by handling them briefly every day starting from a few minutes and extending the duration gradually over time
- Handle your kitten gently ensuring you support their body and hind legs – no picking up and holding by the scruff
- Comfort and stroke your kitten while using words of encouragement to help them feel relaxed
- Any attacking, play fighting or signs of extreme dislike or stress should be responded to appropriately (e.g. if you are bitten firmly say "no" in a deep tone of voice) and put an end to the day's handling by gently placing the kitten on the floor or somewhere comfortable they can relax
- Engage your kitten in regular play with plenty of stimulating toys so you can bond with them and engage them effectively
- Immediately put a stop to any play time if your kitten starts behaving badly or aggressively and go away to another room – they will associate their naughty action with the fun ending
- Understand that different kittens have different personalities and some, by nature, will be less social – give it time, try and bond regularly and never force them to do anything
- Introduce your kitten to people in a calm and quiet environment where those involved can bond and comfort the kitten
- Don't overload your kitten with too much interaction and ensure they have a quiet place to retreat to at their will
- Allow your kitten to explore objects such as boxes and other things that can be played with and investigated safely – your kitten will then learn more about their surroundings and feel more comfortable
- Avoid startling or scaring your kitten with sudden movements, loud noises, scolding and so on – also make any children in the household aware they must be gentle and calm around the kitten

- Let your kitten explore different parts of the house so they become familiar with where noises are coming from and that their environment is safe
- Allow your kitten to approach people instead of the person approaching them
- If your kitten decides to retreat you should let them do so
- Keep introductions and interactions with people, other animals and other potentially 'unknown' and scary things brief to begin with and gradually extend as you go along.

Some kittens may take longer than others during socialisation and there are two effective training techniques you can give your kitten to improve their behaviour. These two approaches are particularly useful for kittens who haven't taken to socialisation well or haven't had a good experience with socialisation. Let's take a look at these two methods Desensitisation: This technique is all about helping your kitten react in a less sensitive way towards objects, animals, people or whatever thing they find scary or stressful.

A scared or stressed kitten is not a happy kitten, so be very vigilant and perform the desensitisation process slowly. It's all about gradual exposure, so start small – introduce your kitten to its fear in a very mild way. For example, if your kitten is scared of visitors invite someone over and let your kitten sit in the same room. Make sure the kitten is a fair distance away from the visitor and ensure they are not exposed for too long a time or they will become highly anxious.

Once your kitten is used to this you can step things up a bit. Try placing the kitten closer to the visitor and make sure the visitor doesn't engage with the kitten just yet. After a time they will begin to learn that visitors are not there to harm them and you can take another step up by allowing your kitten to sit or sleep next to the visitor or perhaps introduce brief interaction by stroking or encouraging talk.

Soon they may be able to play with them or have them sit on their lap. Taking relaxed, manageable steps will ease your kitten into familiarising and accepting other humans.

Counterconditioning: This method is all about noticing what your kitten fears and re-teaching them how to cope with it by altering the fearful feeling to a happier one. Much like desensitisation, this method takes time and patience. For example, if your kitten is scared of loud, energetic children living in the house you can make some changes to alter the kitten's mood. If you start out with desensitisation by putting your kitten in the same room as the children at a distance, you can replace the kitten's memories and feelings of "children are loud and scary" to "every time I see the children I get treats and strokes!" Tell the children to be calmer and quieter at first and let them give your kitten a treat or a new toy. The kids should try doing this on several occasions until your kitten begins to connect meeting children with enjoyable things happening such as eating delicious treats and playing with new and exciting toys.

Both counterconditioning and desensitisation techniques work well when done together. Your kitten will not only be learning the thing they fear is harmless, but that experiencing them can be quite pleasant – this certainly helps them get used to things and, in many regards, improves their behaviour around their ex-fear and their general wellbeing.

CHAPTER 9
the kitten behaviour index

You might find it helpful to understand why your kitten does this or that. Once you know why your kitten behaves in a particular way you can take the steps to understand them or resolve any problems. As kittens can't speak to us, understanding the reasons behind the things they do is important, so here is a little index of common kitten behaviours you can refer to with explanations on why your kitten could be showing a particular behaviour.

Fighting/aggression – A kitten fighting or showing signs of aggression towards other cats or humans could be doing so for many reasons. They could be a male reaching maturity, they could be beginning to become territorial, they could have an underlying behavioural problem or medical condition or they could actually be play fighting which is natural and extremely common. Separate kittens that fight and cause injury to one another and definitely consider neutering when they reach the suitable age. Any other unusual behaviours or abnormalities with health should be investigated by a vet.

Clinginess – Some kittens can be very clingy and follow you around the house. This could be because they're not getting enough social interaction and stimulation from you or in general. Cats are social creatures and certain breeds are more social than others. More attention, play time and affection is being requested from you. A kitten with a play mate, especially another cat, will be happier.

Rolling – Kittens who roll over can be showing you affection and trust. They may also be wishing to gain attention from you. In some cases they might just want their belly rubbed!

Hiding away – Not always a bad thing. Cats are animals who love to explore and find little nooks and crannies they can get themselves into simply because it's fun, comfortable, safe or a good place to nap. A constantly hiding kitten could be scared over a particular situation, animal or person. Do some investigating to find out what it could be. The socialisation process should help this matter and additional housetraining such as desensitisation and counterconditioning is effective.

Rubbing/bunting – A kitten that rubs their face or body against you, otherwise known as bunting, is showing signs of affection, being social or wishing to get your attention. They are also marking you with their scent.

Causing a mess/being destructive – Kittens can be messy, particularly those who are at the pre-housetraining stages. Not being trained or not imitating the mother's behaviour could be behind such a messy kitten. Kittens that cause destruction around the house could also be suffering from separation anxiety when you leave the house and they get bored and lonely. It could also be a sign of seeking attention, being compulsive, not getting enough stimulation, having a natural instinct to use their claws, not being supervised enough or not having enough physical activity in their day to day lives.

Licking or eating household objects – Otherwise known as pica, this behaviour involves your kitten licking or eating non-food objects around the house. This could be because of genetics, an underlying medical condition, malnutrition or unbalanced diet, deficiencies in the diet, boredom or even stress. Because there's a risk of being poisoned, being sick, choking or having an internal blockage you should get this behaviour checked out by a vet, improve their diet and always be vigilant when you see it happening.

Excessive meowing – A kitten who is vocal to excess could be doing so because they're ill, in pain, want to be left alone or are annoyed by too much interaction, they wish to be fed, they want to get attention, they're being social, doing it out of loneliness, a female who is starting to go into season or because they're stressed out.

Sluggishness – Kittens will sleep a lot because they're developing and growing all the time. If you notice your kitten has suddenly become sluggish it might be because they're overtired from too much stimulation or interaction, or it could be because they're ill. In any doubt you should contact your vet.

Hissing or growling – Common signs your kitten is scared, angry or feeling threatened and these are often accompanied by a change in body language. Another reason a kitten might growl is when they are eating - they don't want other cats taking their food – but you don't want to encourage food possessiveness.

Avoiding physical contact – A kitten who walks or runs away or ducks their head to avoid physical contact could be because they have not been properly socialised or they could have had a bad experience with a human that has instilled fear into them. A kitten that avoids your touch when they normally receive it well could simply want their own space at that particular time and not want to be touched.

Playing rough – Kittens playing rough are just behaving as nature intended. They play fight with their mother and siblings from a very young age and playing too rough can naturally be communicated by other cats when the biting gets painful. Cats actually learn from play fighting each other about when they get too rough. If it happens to you nip it in the bud if it gets out of hand.

Begging – A begging kitten might be telling you they want feeding. Kittens are growing so, much like a teenager, they love their food. They can also beg because they've developed a liking for human food and they know you have it. Try to avoid giving in to begging by feeding them more than they should have and try to discourage the feeding of human foods. Cats can sometimes beg as a way to get something from you, such as attention.

Spraying – Older kittens reaching maturity around six months old can spray. Spraying is otherwise known as marking and occurs on vertical surfaces as a form of communication to other cats, a sign of stress or marking territory. It's common in unneutered males, so getting them neutered can put a stop to this behaviour.

Purring – Everyone knows why a kitten purrs: affection, happiness and feeling secure. Some kittens also purr when they're sleeping. Not everybody realises, though, that purring could mean the kitten feels scared or ill. If you notice purring accompanied by unusual behaviour then it could be a sign something is wrong and you need to see the vet.

Hyperactivity – It's common for kittens to play with lots of energy. They are active creatures with instincts to be predatory and playful, so if a kitten is unstimulated and bored it's common for them to want to use up this excess energy. Engage them with toys and play. Unneutered kittens are more likely to be hyperactive, so getting them neutered may calm things down a little bit.

CHAPTER 10
playing and exercise

Kittens need plenty of stimulation in the form of playing with their owners, toys and other cats if possible. Such an energetic creature needs regular activity and as an owner you should set some time aside on a daily basis to ensure you engage with playtime.

Advantages of daily play and exercise:

- Keeps your kitten at a healthy weight
- Strengthens and develops muscles needed to jump, stretch, climb, etc
- Proven to improve health and prevent medical conditions
- A method to help the management of a medical condition
- Keeps them physically and mentally stimulated
- Tackles depression, boredom, anxiety, etc
- Teaches them socialisation skills with other animals and humans
- Improves the bond between you and your kitten
- Well stimulated and exercised kittens are less likely to be destructive

When and how long should I play with my kitten?

Kittens play from a young age and it normally begins from a few weeks old with their siblings. As soon as your kitten is comfortable interacting with you then it's safe to introduce playtime. Remember kittens are small and though their energy levels are high they will need lots of rest and sleep throughout the day. Play with them a few times each day and keep the sessions brief from around 10 to 20 minutes each.

What kinds of play and exercise can I engage my kitten with?

There are all kinds of games you can play to exercise your kitten in a number of ways. Get them running around, pouncing, jumping and tumbling around. Try not to let them overdo it or hurt themselves. Kittens simply adore people trailing a long toy across the floor so they can sink into their predatory instinct and pounce at it. Anything that allows them to be the predator, as they are naturally, that involves pouncing and chasing something.

What toys are the most suitable for my kitten?

As mentioned earlier in this book, you must avoid anything with small parts or strings that a kitten can chew and choke on. When you choose the toys think of it like you're buying them for a small child. Anything small given to your kitten should be supervised during play. Larger and softer toys are the safest as the risk of choking or injury is minimal. To get your kitten pouncing around you should buy some toys that move around, such as wind up mice. Consider buying toys designed to be used with a human, such as a small cuddly toy attached to a long stick you can move around the floor. Leave a few 'extra special' toys away to get out as a treat – this is a great way to reward your kitten for being good or responding well to training. Also consider toys your kitten can keep occupied with by themselves when you're out of the house, e.g. puzzle toys with treats in the middle your kitten can work out how to get to.

Should I let my kitten play outdoors?

Wait until your kitten is old enough to be well socialised first as well as ensuring they are vaccinated and wormed as the outside world puts them at risk. Introduce them to the outdoors in small fragments as it may be a daunting or stressful experience. Such a young cat should be supervised by you the whole time they are outdoors – you don't want them getting hurt, lost, in a fight or anything else that affects their wellbeing. Just keep an eye on them and make sure they can hop back indoors to comfort and safety if they feel unsure.

Play and exercise – useful tips:

Bed time burst: If you want your kitten to settle down to sleep around about the same time as you try a quick play session just beforehand to get rid of that excess energy and tire them out.

Scratching posts and indoor climbing trees: Have at least one, if not more, scratching posts around the house as your kitten will want to stretch and use their claws often. It will prevent them from causing damage to furniture. Kittens will want to jump, climb and see the room from a high level, so a cat climbing tree will do wonders.

Make-shift toys are just as fun: If there are no toys (cats often hide toys and you might have to work hard to find them again!) try a make-shift toy by scrunching up a paper ball or find a large cardboard box and make some holes in it. They love running after thrown toys and some even play fetch. They also love exploring things, plonking themselves into things and hiding or hanging out in exciting places, which is why boxes are so much fun.

Train the kitten to avoid rough play: Kittens can play rough, but when it gets too far and they end up nipping you and causing you injury you should point and say "no". Make sure you speak in a firm and accentuate your "no" in a tone that gets your kitten's attention.

Provide a range of toys: Toys for you to get involved with, toys the kitten can play with when left alone, toys that move, toys with different textures and features. It means they are fully stimulated at any point during the day.

CHAPTER 11
health and medical conditions

It's crucial to know about your kitten's health. This chapter will provide information for those who have a kitten with a medical condition, for those who want to know about the signs of poor health or those who want to know how to manage or prevent medical problems.

Prevention

Prevention is vital to keep your kitten from getting any illnesses that could be averted by taking a few simple steps. It saves your kitten from being sick, feeling uncomfortable or being in pain. Not only this, but it could save you a lot of trouble and a lot of money in future.

Steps to prevent poor health:

- Balanced, healthy diet – do not over or under feed
- Daily exercise which is best done by playing with humans
- Regular visits to the vet for check-ups and vaccinations
- Flea and worming treatment when instructed

- A safe and clean environment to live in, rest in, play in, eat in, etc
- Regular care such as grooming, claw clipping, ear cleaning and bathing, depending on the breed
- Attending to any medical problems such as making the disabled kitten's bed, food bowl and everything else it needs access to easy to get to
- Ensuring that if your kitten needs to take medicine that it's given correctly and on time as advised by your vet
- Providing plenty of interaction, comfort and mental and physical nourishment
- Neutering if advised by the vet

It's very important your kitten's vaccinations are on time and up to date. Vaccinations prevent your kitten from getting nasty diseases, infections or viruses, some of which are very serious.

Recognising poor health or illness

Noticing the signs is another vital thing to be aware of. If you see something that's not quite right with your kitten, you can act quickly and get it attended to faster – this is important because it increases the chance of your kitten recovering. For signs of a healthy kitten refer to chapter two on 'Choosing Your Kitten' where a list is provided on what signs show your kitten is in good health.

Signs of poor health and illness:

- Diarrhoea
- Vomiting
- Lethargy
- Loss of appetite
- Immobility, stiffness, stillness or problems with limbs
- Poor coat condition that is dull, unclean, infested or bald in patches
- Discharge from the ears, eyes, nose or rear
- Swellings and inflammation anywhere around the body
- The third eyelid showing
- Eliminating more frequently or less frequently than normal
- Being under or overweight
- Difficulty breathing

- Excessive scratching or head shaking
- Sores on the skin
- Inflamed gums, yellowed teeth and halitosis (bad breath)
- Discomfort when eliminating, particularly by straining and vocalising
- Sudden signs of reclusiveness, lack of interest in play and interaction, being persistently scared, stressed or anxious

These are just some common signs, but there are many more symptoms belonging to a long list of medical conditions. The easiest way to notice any signs of illness is to make it a routine to check your kitten regularly by getting them weighed, looking at their eyes, ears, mouth and fur and monitoring their behaviour, habits and physical health. You'll get a picture quite quickly of what is normal so it's easier to recognise that something isn't right. If you do notice anything unusual you must see your vet immediately.

Treating poor health and illness

Diagnosis should be kept to the professionals. Once your vet makes a diagnosis they will be able to tell you the suitable treatment for the illness. It can be any number of things – it could simply be advice on making adjustments or improvements such as changing your kitten's diet, fixing up a wound, prescribing medication, performing surgery, giving the kitten a vaccine, treating fleas or parasites and so on. It really depends on what is diagnosed.

Obviously the professionals deal with treatment, but sometimes particular treatments need the understanding and co-operation of the owner. Take advice seriously, so if you're requested to change the kitten's diet or give them more exercise then do so or it could affect their wellbeing drastically. In some instances, you might be asked to administer medication. The vet would normally show you how to do this and you should remember that some kittens are easy to give medicines to and some are very difficult. Here is a quick guide:

Note: *Be careful when giving medication by being observant, trying not to block your kitten's nose with your fingers and take care not to choke them. Always check with your vet upon receiving a prescription on which is the best way to give that specific medicine*

Giving tablets with a syringe: A syringe, or pill pusher, is a specialised syringe that administers tablets. They can be used to pop the tablet right at the back of your kitten's mouth to help them eat it. Kittens would otherwise sniff the tablet and not want to take it. A good trick is to place a treat on the pill holder of the syringe, push it just a little bit in their mouth but not too far and let them chew and enjoy it. Repeat this a few times so they get used to the syringe and learn that what you are giving them tastes nice. After a few treats have been given pop the tablet on the syringe and push it into their mouth, but a little further than the treats went so the kitten doesn't taste the bitterness as much. Sometimes the tablet will fall out and you will need to start the process again. Your kitten might refuse the tablet, so try popping it in accompanied with a treat at the same time. To avoid choking you can use a syringe with water inside to help them swallow.

Giving tablets by hand: Often a tricky method that can lead to the kitten wanting to get away from you or not want to keep still. The best way is to try a position where the kitten is held down gently – try kneeling behind your kitten and having them face away from you or try getting someone else to help you keep them still. Try not to startle them too much. Put your thumb and middle or index fingers onto the corners of their mouth and press gently to enable the mouth to open. Tilt their head upwards and pop the tablet far into the mouth – not too far or they may choke. Manually close their mouth and keep it closed. Hopefully the kitten should swallow. You can adopt this position to administer the tablet with the pill pusher syringe if you'd prefer.

Giving medicine in food: Some people prefer the less hands-on approach of placing or crushing the medication into the kitten's meals. The downside here is that the kitten may be able to taste the bitterness of the medicine and reject their food. Not only could the food be wasted, but the vital medication could be wasted too, which is problematic if you strictly need a set amount. Some cat owners advise that crushing a pill into a moreish, lickable food your kitten will enjoy such as cream cheese is effective. Alternatively, some brands of kitten foods make treats with holes in the centre where pills can be hidden.

Giving liquid, gel or paste-like medicines: Not all medicines come in pill form. Some come in liquid forms such as gels. Or you may crush tablets into a paste-like form. These are normally easier ways for kittens to digest, but putting it in food or in a bowl by itself isn't always a success. Any pastes or gels might be worth giving somewhere your kitten is more likely to lick or routinely clean – try putting it on their paws, on their lips or even wipe some on your finger. Some liquids are best given with a spoon or syringe. Ear or eye drops should be administered while you hold your kitten's head upwards and should be kept up a few moments after to stop the drops dribbling out.

Common medical conditions kittens are susceptible to

A young and healthy kitten would normally have nothing to worry about, but there are many common medical problems that even a kitten can suffer from. In fact, there are certain illnesses kittens can be more prone to getting than older cats.

Let's look at a few examples of problems your kitten could suffer from:

Important note: *Don't assume anything can clear up by itself. If your kitten shows any signs of illness, even signs that are not mentioned below, you must book an immediate appointment with the vet.*

Allergies
An often common problem for kittens. Kittens can be allergic to various things such as cow's milk, household objects such as plants or cleaning products, fleas, mites, pollen, specific foods, certain scents and so on. Signs of an allergy include runny eyes, excessive scratching, dry skin, sneezing or coughing, diarrhoea, vomiting, swelling around the face or head, hair loss or sores.

 Depending on the cause, your vet will likely recommend changes to the diet, changes to the environment such as keeping chemicals well away from the kitten's reach or a course of medication such as antihistamines, topical treatments or steroids.
 ·

Fleas, mites, worms or lice

Not a pleasant problem and can be common in any cat, particularly ones who roam outdoors. Your vet can recommend a suitable treatment, some of which are to be applied regularly as a prevention method. Cleaning bedding, blankets and regular vacuum cleaning is also recommended. Be sure to brush and comb your kitten often. Kittens can be susceptible to roundworms and tapeworms, so speak to your vet for a treatment suitable for kittens. Signs of parasites include excessive scratching and licking, sore skin from scratching, head shaking, swelling of the ear with a blood blister (aural haematoma), specks in the fur and rice-like bits found in faeces, in the kitten's bedding or around their anus. Mothers can pass on parasites to their litter, e.g. through their milk, so it's important to treat all cats.

Internal hairballs

Most common in longhaired kittens where the loose fur is ingested from the kitten grooming itself. The fur collects up causing internal upset, coughing up, constipation, vomiting, gagging or diarrhoea and can even be quite serious, so regular grooming is strongly advised to prevent this. If needed, your vet can prescribe treatment.

Upper respiratory infection

Also called 'cat flu' and is well-known in kittens. The symptoms are more severe compared to older cats and it can potentially be very serious. Symptoms include sneezing, nose discharge, eye discharge, inflamed eyelids, coughing, high temperature, lethargy and poor appetite. It's known to be very infectious, so other cats can pass on the infection or are at risk of getting it. Your vet needs to investigate the cause, such as infection from feline herpes virus or feline calicivirus. Antibiotics, decongestants, anti-viral drugs or injections such as interferons may be used as treatment.

Feline calicivirus infection

Common and a major cause of cat flu. Potentially very serious, particularly in kittens, and highly contagious. The virus is also associated with health problems such as gingivitis and joint inflammation, otherwise known as arthritis. Improved diets, improved hygiene, decongestants and antibiotics are common treatments given by vets. Vaccinations are strongly advised.

Feline herpes virus

Closely linked with feline calicivirus and again, is a main cause behind cat flu. Very contagious and can be very serious. It's associated with skin inflammation, keratitis and conjunctivitis. Antiviral drugs, antiviral topical medicine, antibiotics and decongestants are common treatments used by vets, with a vaccination strongly advised.

Feline leukaemia virus

The two viruses mentioned above along with feline leukaemia virus are three extremely good reasons why you must get your kitten vaccinated. It can be fatal and is contagious given from one cat to another. Kittens can also get it from their mother. The virus doesn't always have noticeable symptoms, but typical signs could include fever, poor appetite, weight loss, sneezing, lethargy, running eyes or nose, diarrhoea or vomiting. As the signs are vague, you must see your vet if you notice any. Improved environment and diet, keeping the cat indoors and carrying out recommendations and treatments by your vet will help, but there is no outright cure.

Feline Panleukopenia/Feline enteritis/Feline distemper

A fourth and, again, very important reason to vaccinate your kitten. This is an extremely serious and very contagious disease belonging to the Parvovirus group. It's most common in feral cat colonies and in kittens. Mothers with the disease can often pass it onto their litters. Common symptoms include dehydration, lethargy, poor appetite, vomiting, diarrhoea, fever, depression or sudden death. Your vet will find ways to increase the chances of your kitten being able to fight it off (e.g. vitamin injections, antibiotics, improved diet and living conditions, blood transfusions, etc), but there is no outright cure and no guarantee of survival.

Diarrhoea or vomiting

A common mistake to assume diarrhoea or vomiting or a combination of both is nothing. Kittens are more likely to be sick or have diarrhoea and multiple illnesses have them as a core symptom, so it's very important to notify your vet if it persists. Common causes include stress or anxiety, parasites, changes in diet, viral infections, bacterial infections, hairballs, food allergies, dehydration, bad food, diseases involving the bowels, kidneys or liver, colitis, a reaction to being on medication, ingestion of foreign body or non-foods, pancreatitis and many others.

Improvements to diet, access to plenty of water, improved hygiene or various treatments such as medications are known to help, but it really depends on the cause. Both problems can be caused by non-serious illnesses, but they can also be caused by something far more serious, so see your vet.

Constipation
If you notice they defecate less than normal or you notice them strain in their litter tray without any signs of faeces, the chances are it's constipation. A kitten suffering from change in diet or dehydration is likely to get constipation. As more serious problems could be behind severe constipation it's important to visit your vet if your kitten doesn't defecate in 48 hours, particularly if it's combined with other symptoms such as vomiting.

Conjunctivitis
Involves inflammation around the eye with common symptoms of swollen eyelids, pinkness and eye discharge that is either watery, or in severe cases, a thick mucus. Your vet needs to examine the eyes and treatment could involve topical medicines, antibiotics or eye drops depending on the severity. Regular gentle cleansing around the eye may also be recommended.

Anaemia
There could be many causes behind anaemia such as long-term exposure to fleas, worms or ticks, poor red blood cell production, vitamin deficiencies or an underlying disease or illness. An even more serious problem is feline infectious anaemia where the kitten's immune system attempts to destroy the parasites involved but destroys red blood cells as a result. Symptoms include weakness, pale gums, poor appetite, jaundice, weight loss, inflamed lymph nodes, sleeping more than normal, increased breathing and heart rate and fever. Consult your vet about the safe and correct removal of ticks and suitable flea treatments. Antibiotics, diet changes, other medications and blood transfusions are common treatments given by vets.

Fading kitten syndrome
A name given to a group of symptoms and is more known with feral cats. Kittens can often die suddenly from when they are just a few weeks old up until around nine to twelve weeks old. Mothers often abandon one of their kittens or don't have the good health to look after and provide for them as normal. Diseases and complications from parasites are other causes behind sudden death in kittens.

Symptoms include below expected weight, lack of activity, discoloured gums, weakness and inability to keep warm. Early intervention such as warmth food supplements from their owners can save the kitten from incoming death, so remember to look out for the early signs and act swiftly. As it is closely linked with the mother cat, pregnant cats or mothers with a litter should be checked by the vet, particularly ones showing signs of poor health.

Feline infectious peritonitis
Caused by the feline coronavirus, which many cats will have contact with in their lives without any real harm. This particular strain, however, is a mutation and is more common in kittens because their immune systems are not as strong as adult cats. It is contagious and common signs are vague, such as diarrhoea or sneezing. This is why these sort of symptoms need to be addressed by a vet for specific testing to diagnose FIP. Later symptoms are called 'wet' and dry' – wet involving a build-up of fluids in the abdomen or chest along with difficulty breathing, or dry involving inflammatory lesions around various organs in the body, fever, lethargy, anaemia, depression, weight loss, poor appetite, changes to mobility and gait, paralysis, loss of vision and can cause problems with the nervous system, eyes, brain, kidneys or liver. There is no cure and it can be fatal, so your vet will need to look at supportive methods and euthanasia.

Feline immunodeficiency virus
This virus is similar to HIV in humans and the most common cause of infection is through cat bites. It cannot be caught by humans and isn't necessarily something you need to worry about regarding your kitten as middle-aged outdoor cats are the most likely to get infected. It's worth mentioning, however, as infected mothers could pass it on to their litter through her milk. It affects the immune system which later can lead to secondary diseases such as gum infections, urinary tract infections, respiratory infections, conjunctivitis, etc. There is no cure and your vet is likely to focus on treating the secondary problems the immune system isn't dealing with properly.

Heartworm
Involves the infection of a parasite spread by mosquitoes that can affect the heart, lungs and the arteries of a cat. Though heartworm isn't more likely to occur in kittens, it is generally considered that kittens are less likely to survive it than an adult cat.

Symptoms include wheezing and coughing, breathing difficulties, poor appetite, panting, lethargy, vomiting, weight loss and possible heart murmur. It's known to be a cause behind respiratory diseases.

Though there is no cure readily available, your vet will most likely want to monitor your kitten regularly and see if they can fight it off by themselves. Support treatments can be given if problems occur due to heartworm.

Ringworm

No worms are involved this time! It is, in fact, a contagious fungal disease likely to infect the skin, fur and claws. Kittens are at risk of ringworm and other pets and humans are at risk with an infected cat in the household. Typical signs involve red ring-shaped skin lesions, bald patches within the fur, general redness and dry and flaky skin.

Like with any other contagious infection you should clean areas that have had direct contact with the infected cat. Mild cases are normally treated with medicated anti-fungal shampoos or ointments. Medication may be prescribed and courses of medication can be lengthy due the resilience of ringworm.

Abscesses

Kittens love to play rough, but this may inevitably end in injury that involves sharp teeth and claws embedding bacteria under the skin that can often get trapped and inflame.

This is when abscesses can develop. Signs of abscesses include swelling, redness, hotness, pain, patches of baldness, immobility, fever and poor appetite. Your vet can treat it by hygienically and carefully draining it and prescribing a course of antibiotics.

A few things to remember…

- Many medical issues could be secondary diseases with another underlying cause, so it's vital to get your kitten checked by a vet
- A book is useful, but it's not a substitute for going to the vet – any signs of poor health or illness needs to be looked at by a professional first hand

- Kittens are more prone to certain illnesses because specific ones can be passed on by the mother to her litter, so if the mother has a medical condition your kittens need to be examined and she should be neutered to prevent further litters being in bad health
- Having more than one cat or pet in the household means there is an increased risk of contagious infections being caught from one pet to an other – if one pet is has a disease, get the others checked too
- Some diseases can be infectious with bacteria present in saliva and faeces. A good way to prevent diseases reoccurring or to prevent them from being contagious to other pets would be to practice thorough and regular hygiene, e.g. regular vacuum cleaning of bedding and carpets, washing bedding, cleaning food and water bowls each time after use, clearing litter trays every day, etc.

CHAPTER 11
the kitten conclusion

Though kittens are unbearably adorable and small, they will grow and grow and grow. Time will fly and before you know it they will be adult cats with a greater desire for independence. The whole reason they get to this stage is because of you – an owner who looks after them well and gives them everything they need to be a healthy and happy cat.

It's unlikely that anything will go badly wrong if you're attentive to your kitten's wellbeing. He or she will love you for it by being affectionate, loyal, playful and bringing a whole lot of joy into your life. In fact, some say that having a cat is actually good for your wellbeing, too!

The most important thing required to get your kitten through kittenhood is understanding: an understanding of how they may be feeling, how they perceive the world, how and why they behave, how their biology works and what is needed to look after them properly. You don't need to become an expert, you just need a sense of awareness.

You may still have questions popping up in your head and many of the answers might be given by simply spending time with your kitten and learning about them. Always remember, too, that books are helpful, but they cannot look at your individual circumstance – your vet, however, can and it's vital to involve them every step of the way to ensure your kitten is going great. They are also helpful in answering any questions you have, so please don't feel like you are wasting their time – it's what they are there for. Hopefully by this point the guide will have given you at least some awareness on what you need to do before you choose a kitten and what should happen once they are with you. Further information can be found online, with many cat-based organisations and veterinary hospitals having websites containing a wealth of detail and advice. Many pet owners revel in the delights of online forums where you can share your experiences and relate to other kitten owners.

One last piece of advice is to remember about safety nets – not actual safety nets, but back-ups that are there just in case. In this instance it's pet insurance. It's a confusing thing to research and find a reputable insurer and nobody can advise on which is the best one because people often recommend or condemn from their individual experiences. Many kittens come with a limited period of free pet insurance, but always remember to keep them covered throughout their lives. It may cost money, but the alternative could be costlier and a lot more heart-breaking. So, are you ready to introduce your dream kitten into your life? What are they going to be called? That's something we cannot help you with! Before you take that first step just ask yourself whether you are ready, whether you can afford it, whether you have all the right equipment to keep them happy and comfortable, whether you have the spare time to interact and play with them and so on. This isn't meant to throw you off. In fact, it's quite straightforward for a responsible person to be ready for a new pet. If you're serious and dedicated about wanting a kitten you should be very confidently answering "yes!" to all those factors. Any doubt in your mind may mean you are not ready for a kitten just yet, and that's okay. All it means is you need more time or a change of circumstances before it's the right time and if you really want it, that day will come and the right kitten will come along too. The last thing anyone or any kitten needs is to be rehomed and then rehomed again.

All that's left to be said now is good luck and you're guaranteed a wonderful and rewarding experience inviting a kitten into your life, so enjoy it, love your kitten and you'll get a whole load of love back!

Made in the USA
Las Vegas, NV
15 June 2023